how NOT to get
PENALTY
points
in
Northern Ireland

how NOT to get PENALTY points in Northern Ireland

peter prenter ll.b.

APPLETREE PRESS

Acknowledgement
The author would like to thank the RUC for their kind
assistance in the compilation of this book.

First published in 2000
by Appletree
The Old Potato Station
14 Howard Street South
Belfast BT7 1AP

Tel: +44 (0) 28 90 243074
Fax: +44 (0) 28 90 246756
Web Site: www.appletree.ie
E-mail: reception@appletree.ie

Text copyright © Paul Donnelly

How Not To Get Penalty Points in Northern Ireland

A catalogue record for this book is
available from the British Library

ISBN 0-86281-810-9

9 8 7 6 5 4 3 2 1

FOREWORD

Our driving licence touches most facets of our lives.

Penalty points incurred can put you off the road yet most people know little or nothing about the penalty points system or the method that is used for detection of alleged offences.

Points imposed affect insurance premiums:

– between 7 and 9 points and insurance premiums can increase by 50% to 100%

– specialist insurance policies, such as taxi drivers can have premiums increased dramatically on the imposition of only 3 points.

It is possible to beat the system temporarily. But as soon as loopholes are discovered legislators invariably move to close them.

The safest option is to stay on the right side of the penalty points system and to keep driving safely.

The Government have recently announced that the penalty for Endorsable tickets will increase from £40 to £60, and Non-Endorsable tickets from £20 to £30. However, they have yet to announce the date from which these increases will take effect.

CONTENTS

THE PENALTY
POINTS SYSTEM

THE PENALTY POINTS SYSTEM

The Penalty Points System came into force in Northern Ireland on the 1st October 1997.

Police in Northern Ireland now issue on average six thousand points each month. That figure does not include points awarded by the Courts.

A penalty points total amounting to twelve points or more within a three-year period means a minimum ban of six months.

A new driver need only accrue six points in two years to face a ban.

Each award of points lasts for three years.

For example:

01.07.2000 given 3 points

01.08.2000 given another 4 points

Total as of 02.08.00 = 7 points

01.07.2003 3 points "expire". Total now = 4 points.

The penalty points system is a three-tier system.

The purpose of the penalty points provisions is to encourage the Courts to impose periods of disqualification on offenders who are guilty of a number of minor offences in their own right.

It should be noted that the police do not disqualify drivers. Once a total of twelve points is accumulated within three years then a driving licence will be revoked.

If, for example, a driver has nine points on his licence and is stopped by the police for an alleged offence then the matter must be reported to the Courts.

Motorists can receive penalty points from three routes:

1. Endorsable Ticket – stopped by police for a traffic offence and issued an Endorsable Fixed Penalty Ticket at the roadside.

2. Conditional Offer – detected by police speeding or breaching a traffic sign, not stopped at the time, but receive a Conditional Offer of 3 Penalty Points and a £40 penalty in the post ("offer" seems an inappropriate term but that is the terminology used!).

3. Magistrates Court – summoned to a court and penalty points imposed by the court

Police issue 2 types of tickets.

1. Endorsable Fixed Penalty Ticket (EFPT)

2. Non-Endorsable Fixed Penalty Ticket (NEFPT)

TICKETS

TICKETS

This is by far the most common route for motorists to get penalty points.

An "Endorsable" ticket gives you an endorsement on your licence of 3 points and requires you to pay a £40 penalty. Police officers cannot accept the payment, it must go to the Fixed Penalty Office in the centre of Belfast either in the post or you can take it in person.

Police will only issue one Endorsable ticket per driver per stop.

If there appears to be more than one offence then the police must issue a Summons and proceed to court.

Non–Endorsable fixed penalty ticket

- 3 points

- £40 penalty

- Only one ticket per stop.

To be able to accept an Endorsable ticket you must:

– Have a Northern Ireland licence (a licence issued anywhere other than Coleraine cannot be accepted, for example Swansea).

– Be able to surrender both parts of your licence either to the police officer at the time or within 7 days to any police station in N.I.

– The licence must be valid, if it has expired by one day it cannot be accepted.

Endorsable Fixed Penalty Tickets

Why accept an Endorsable ticket?

Endorsable fixed penalty ticket

Because the only alternative to an Endorsable ticket is a Magistrates Court appearance and all that entails.

– If you wish to contest the alleged offence then opt for a court hearing.

– If you opt to accept a ticket then:

  1. Your driving licence should be readily available.

– If you opt to attend court you must have your licence available otherwise you run the risk of:

  1. Being convicted of a further offence.

  2. Having your licence suspended until it is produced to the court.

Once you have been issued your Endorsable ticket… comply with the deadlines

• Hand your licence in within the 7 days, if you have not already given your licence to the police offcer.

- Pay the £40 penalty well within the 21 days. If all parts are not complied with in time it automatcally defaults to a Magistrates Court.

Surprisingly, a lot of people risk ending up with more penalty points than they need to through complacency.

Driver and Vehicle Licensing at Coleraine will give you a full Northern Ireland licence in exchange for a full licence issued in Swansea or a licence issued in one of the following countries:-

European Union Member States:
Austria, Belgium, Denmark, Finland, France, Germany, Greece, Ireland, Italy, Luxembourg, Portugal, Spain, Sweden, The Netherlands

European Economic Areas:
Iceland, Liechtenstein, Norway

Other Countries:
Australia, Barbados, British Virgin Islands, Cyprus, Gibraltar, Hong Kong, Japan, Kenya, Malta, New Zealand, Singapore, Switzerland, Zimbabwe

There are a couple of surprising countries within this list and two surprising omissions, the USA and Canada. For some reason Driver and Vehicle Licencing in the UK will not issue a full UK licence in exchange for an American or Canadian licence. I have no idea why.

Getting Your Licence Back

Once you have surrendered your licence it usually will be back to you within the month. But the process will not start until the licence is handed in. Therefore, handing it to the police officer who stops you will be the quickest method of getting it back.

The payment is the second stage that has to be complied with. If you pay by cheque, the cheque can take up to 10 days to clear. The Fixed Penalty Office will not release the Endorsed licence until the payment has cleared. If you attend the office in person and pay cash, the licence will be released that much quicker.

To have your licence returned quickly

• Surrender it to the police officer that stops you.

• Attend the Fixed Penalty Office in person and pay cash.

Non-Endorsable Fixed Penalty Tickets

This ticket is a monetary penalty only, there are no points with this ticket.

At present it is a £20 penalty.

The majority of these tickets are issued for minor parking offences. However, there are a multitude of other offences it is issued for.

Common examples are:

– Failure to wear a seat-belt

– Unlawful use of lamp: this is primarily issued for use of fog lamps in fine weather. The problem with fog lights are that the lenses are designed to help the light cut through fog. When they are used in fine weather the only thing they cut through are the retinas of other drivers, therefore causing a hazard. Front fog lights it would seem have become some thing of a fashion accessory.

– Driver unable to have proper control of vehicle: used for very minor cases of use of mobile phones. If you get one of these for using your mobile you are, relatively speaking, lucky. For details of what could have happened to you check out the section specifically on mobiles.

– Incorrect form of registration mark: any deviation from the normal size and colour on your number plate will leave you exposed to a ticket. Number plates are maybe not the best place to show the artistic side of your character.

– Use of horn offences: using your horn when you are not meant to. Taxi drivers beware...

– No taxi roof sign: again one for the taxi driver.

– Failing to drive in the nearside lane: yes, you can get a ticket for sitting in the outside lane. The inside lane would of course need to be clear. Some people fail to realise that they are meant to drive in the nearside lane.

– Overtaking in the inside lane: so don't be tempted to "undertake" that person sitting in the outside lane driving at 20mph. I know they shouldn't be there but at the moment you are in the right and they are in line for a ticket. Keep on the legal high ground and hope for a Traffic Branch patrol…

– Turning right without signalling: pretty self-explanatory. If you make a right-hand turn without indicating it could be rather dangerous if another motorist was about to overtake your vehicle.

– Defective light: this could be a side light, a dipped beam, a tail light or even a brake light. Brake light is probably the most seriously viewed, so this is the most likely one to get a ticket for. When they blow get them fixed the same day, they are a lot cheaper than a £20 ticket…

These are only a handful of the offences that the Non-Endorsable Ticket can be issued for. The full range is too numerous to list but usually they are for static or non-driving offences.

POLICE SPEED
ENFORCEMENT

POLICE SPEED ENFORCEMENT

Guidelines

ACPO (Association of Chief Police Officers), which is basically the Chief Constables of all the UK police forces, getting together and deciding how best to enforce the speed limits.

They pass on their guidelines to all the UK police forces. Each force has a Policy Executive Committee which in turn passes the guidelines on to the force.

The present guidelines are as follows:

(The 10% grace is in recognition of the fact that all production vehicle speedometer may show a small error of less than 10%)

Speed Limit	Verbal Warning	Endorsable Tickets	Summons
Roads less than 60mph	0 – 10mph over the limit	11 – 25mph over the limit	26mph + over the limit
Roads of 60mph	up to 10% + 2mph over the limit (up to 68mph)	69 – 85mph	86mph +
Roads of 70mph (including motorways)	up to 10% + 2mph over the limit (up to 79mph)	80 – 95mph	96mph +

These are guidelines only, they are not legally binding on the police. A Constable enforcing speed limits may decide a different course of action is more appropriate for that road at that particular time. These ACPO guidelines have faced a legal challenge by a member of the public in England. Not because of their severity but because they were not severe enough! Consequently, ACPO have drawn up new draft proposals and, if adopted, we could shortly see motorists:

- Getting 3 points from 36mph onwards in a 30mph zone (rigid adherence to the 10%+2mph rule)

- Being taken to court at just 20mph over the speed limit in a 30mph zone. So travelling at 50mph in a 30mph zone would mean a court appearance and prosecution rather than a simple ticket!

Proposed ACPO Guidelines

The new guideline table could look like this:-

Speed Limit	VerbalWarning	EndorsableTicket	Summons
30	31–35mph	36–49mph	50mph onward
40	41–46mph	47–65mph	66mph onward
50	51–57mph	58–75mph	76mph onward
60	61–68mph	69–85mph	86mph onward
70	71–79mph	80–95mph	96mph onward

These new guidelines, if adopted, would result in a lot more motorists obtaining penalty points and a lot more reaching the dreaded 12 point total.

Police Speed Detection Devices

The most common speed detection devices presently used by police are:

- Radar
- VASCAR
- Pro-Laser II
- LTI 20 20 Laser
- Mobile Speed Camera Enforcement
- GATSO Cameras

Radar

A handheld device, which uses radio waves to measure speed. It uses the Doppler principle, which states that if you transmit a "known" frequency at a moving object and a reflected signal is received, the difference

between the two frequencies is directly proportional to the speed of the object.

It has its limitations with very heavy traffic, an area in which the Laser devices excel.

Vascar

Visual Average Speed Computer And Recorder, its title gives you some idea how this piece of equipment works. It is an on-board computer which can, by operation of the toggle switches that you can see on

the front of the unit, be used to measure the time taken by a vehicle over a distance which it measures and then gives you an average speed for that target vehicle.

The VASCAR unit is linked to the transmission of the vehicle; this enables it to accurately measure distances and also continually give a reading of the police vehicle's current speed. You may have seen programmes that feature actual recordings from police vehicle cameras. On the bottom of the screen you may have noticed the police vehicle's speed. This comes from the VASCAR unit, which is linked to the recording equipment.VASCAR can be used to measure the average speed of a target vehicle in a number of ways.

1. Police vehicle following target vehicle.

2. Target vehicle following the police vehicle.

3. When the target vehicle overtakes the police vehicle or visa-versa (usually this would be an unmarked police vehicle. However, there have been documented cases of some drivers overtaking marked police vehicles at high speed).

4. The Preferred method. This method involves the police vehicle being stationary. The operator has sight of a measured stretch of road. The operator then merely has to measure the time that the target vehicle takes to cover that distance and VASCAR does the rest, giving the average speed of the target vehicle.

This is a very versatile means of speed detection.

Pro-laser II

The Pro-Laser II is usually tripod mounted.

The operator looks through an optical sight on the top of the laser and uses red cross-hairs in the sight to target particular vehicles. The operator then pulls a trigger, which emits a laser beam at the target vehicle. The equipment will then give a reading of the vehicle's speed. It takes a fraction of a second for the laser to obtain this reading.

Laser uses invisible light waves, motorists will not see any emissions from the equipment.

Because the wavelength of these lightwaves is so much shorter than microwaves they can be readily focused into an extremely narrow beam for exact target identification. Thus laser can accurately pick out a vehicle from a line of traffic.

The Pro-Laser can measure the speed of vehicles approaching or moving away from it. The speed of receding vehicles will be prefixed with a minus sign. The equipment can measure the speeds of vehicles over a kilometre away. The usual working distances are shorter than this but the police are still taking your speed long before you can see them. The Pro-Laser also automatically measures the distance to the target vehicle in feet.

- Takes a fraction of a second to take reading

- Can take a speed reading over a kilometre away

- Can take speed readings of vehicles going in either direction

- Can pick one car out of a line of traffic

- Automatically measures the distance in feet

LTI 20 20 Laser

The LTI 20 20 is usually tripod mounted but there is a lighter version that has been specifically designed for handheld use.

The operator uses a magnified scope on the top of the laser to target vehicles. A red dot in the centre of the scope is placed on the front of the on-coming vehicle and the trigger depressed.

As with the Pro-Laser the LTI 20 20 takes a fraction of a second, 0.3 of a second to be precise, for the laser to obtain the reading.

The LTI 20 20 and the Pro-Laser have very similar specifications.

The LTI 20 20 can measure the speed of a vehicle approaching or going away from it. The speed reading of a receding vehicle will be prefixed with a minus sign. The equipment can measure the speed of a vehicle up to a kilometre away.

The LTI 20 20 is so sophisticated that it also automatically measures the distance to the target vehicle in metres.

- It can take speed readings of vehicles going in either direction

- It can pick out a car from a line of traffic

- It can take a reading up to a kilometre away

- Automatically measures the distance in metres

- LTI 20 20 is often used in association with the speed camera in N.I.

Speed camera enforcement

The only speed camera enforcement in N.I. are vehicular mounted cameras. They use a laser usually the LTI 20 20 connected to recording equipment.

The speed camera vehicle must be stationary to record offenders' speeds. It records a video, not stills as some people believe. They do not normally stop vehicles at the time of detection.

They operate within the ACPO guidelines and offer Endorsable tickets to some motorists and others, who are more than 25mph over the speed limit, will receive a Summons to the Magistrates Court.

The mechanism for doing this is as follows:

On returning to their base the Camera Enforcement Team identify which vehicles were in excess of the speed limit and by how much.

– Notice sent to last registered owner within 14 days. Each of the vehicle registration numbers is checked and the Last Registered Owners (LRO) receive a Notice Of Intention To Prosecute in the post. This will arrive within 14 Days.

The Notice will state "it is intended to take proceedings against the driver for excess speed".

At this stage it may tell you the speed the vehicle was travelling or it may just tell you the speed limit for the road. If it tells you the speed of the vehicle, it is most likely over the 25mph ceiling and the driver is bound for court. If it only informs you of the speed limit it is good news (relatively speaking) and a Conditional Offer is the next possible stage.

It then states the allegation is supported by photographic evidence

What Do You Do?

The Notice requires you as the owner of the car to give the details of the driver at the time of the offence. This may well be you.

At this stage you might be thinking "Oh yeah? Well I'm not telling". Wrong. Under Article 177 of the Road Traffic (NI) Order if you do not supply this information within 21 days of the date of the Notice you could be given the penalty points and the fine even if you were not driving! So do not just ignore the Notice because you know you were not driving.

- Return the required details within 21 days. After you fill in the details on the reverse and return it, you will either receive a further letter giving a Conditional Offer or a Summons to the Magistrates Court.

- Or try to contest this power under the Human Rights Act.

Conditional offer

The Conditional Offer will offer to settle the case by way of an endorsement on your licence of 3 penalty points and a penalty of £40 – the same penalty as if you had been stopped at the roadside and offered an Endorsable ticket.

You will have to enclose both parts of your licence and payment of £40 to the Fixed Penalty Office within 28 days from the date of the Conditional Offer. Failure to comply with any of the conditions will result in a Summons being issued for the Magistrates Court.

- Return conditional offer with licence and £40 within 28 days.

- Summons will take about a month to arrive and give a date in about 2 month's time for a court hearing.

GATSO Cameras

GATSO speed cameras are springing up all over mainland Great Britain.

The GATSO measures speed by a radar beam that is constantly emitted across the road. Cars breaking the beam bounce the signal back and the frequency determines the vehicle's speed.

The GATSO camera takes two photographs so the vehicle's speed can be double checked using the white lines that are painted on the road.

Don't think just because you over on the mainland for a holiday you are exempt, you are not. Many a holiday maker from N.I. has received something unwelcome in the post upon their return.

Holders of N.I. driving licences cannot get a Conditional Offer.

If you are unlucky enough to get caught by a GATSO, I'm afraid you will have to check out the availability of any HSS offers to get back over for a court appearance.

Police power to demand details of the driver

The Camera Enforcement system relies on the power of police to demand the details of the driver at the time of the alleged offence from the Last Registered Owner (LRO). In February 2000 at a ruling in a court in Fife, Scotland, Scottish judges held that this power was contrary to European human rights law. They ruled that the threat of prosecution contravenes a suspect's right against self-incrimination, effectively destroying the police's power to demand the name of the driver from the registered owner of the vehicle.This ruling only related to Scotland and Colin Boyd QC, Scotland's Solicitor General, was given leave to appeal on behalf of the Government.

The decision was followed in Birmingham but the matter is as yet undecided in Northern Ireland.

In Northern Ireland, for example, a local politician attempted to run this defence but was unsuccessful. This position may change now that the Human Rights Act is fully implemented and a court could decide against the legislation on the basis of the right against self-incrimination, enshrined in the European Convention on Human Rights.

Therefore whilst the rulings in the above local courts are important ones, it is yet to be successfully applied in Northern Ireland and as has been clearly seen there are risks involved in running this defence.

The prosecuting authorities intend to continue to push this point and no doubt will try to prosecute people for failing to give information under Road Traffic Legislation.

What if a summons is issued? The matter will progress to court.

Obtaining the services of a Solicitor is always a good idea. However, some defendants worry about the cost. A defendant, especially in a Road Traffic offence, is not obliged to instruct a solicitor.

Most times, Legal Aid will not be granted for a road traffic offence unless it involves the risk of imprisonment (e.g. driving whilst disqualified).

Arrive at the Magistrates Court at the time indicated on the Summons and speak to the staff on duty. They will point you to the lists for each court (there may be several different courts in the one building). Go to the court number which you are listed for. Near the front of the court you will see a Police Inspector; he is presenting the police case against you. Don't be afraid to speak to him, this isn't Perry Mason, this is small potatoes. The court should not be in progress at this time; this is the time for getting things sorted out prior to the Magistrate's arrival. Introduce yourself to the Inspector and tell him what plea you will be entering, i.e. "Guilty" or "Not Guilty", then take a seat in the body of the court.

When the Magistrate enters the court everyone will stand and then sit down when the Magistrate sits. The cases will not necessarily be called in the order they are listed. The guilty pleas are taken first and are usually called by the defence solicitor asking the Magistrate to hear their client's plea. You will see the defence solicitors jockeying for position at the front of the court, they will enter and leave the court with a bow throughout the morning. The solicitors may be representing persons in a number of the courts in and around the same time, so they try to get in and out of each court as quickly as possible.

One of the drawbacks of representing yourself is that your case may be one of the last heard.

When your case is called, stand up, don't worry about looking like a rabbit caught in the headlights of a car, everyone does! The Clerk of the Court (the person doing all the writing, sitting immediately down and in front of the Magistrate) will indicate for you to come to the front of the court. Do not enter the raised area to the left or right of the Magistrate, these areas are either for giving evidence or for the accused in charge cases, not for Summons cases.

You can only speak when you are addressed by the Clerk of the Court or the Magistrate. You only speak to the Magistrate, even if the question is put by the Clerk. Your answer goes to the Magistrate, addressing him or her as "Your Worship". Don't worry, if you treat the Magistrate with respect, he or she will help you along.

Decide what you are going to say beforehand but keep it brief. If you are pleading guilty it won't do your case any harm to indicate that you are aware that you were in the wrong and give some reason for the lapse. It would also be prudent to make the Magistrate aware of any special reason why your licence is important to you or if it may affect your occupation.

Anyone who appears before a Magistrate for excess speed can be awarded anything between 3 and 6 penalty points and a £1000 fine.

Exactly what number of penalty points and what fine you receive is dependent on how fast you were speeding and on any other relevant facts. For example, was it past a school on a school day.

If you have decided to plead "Not Guilty," I would strongly recommend instructing a solicitor.

Remember if you plead not guilty the case will not be heard that day. A date will be set some weeks ahead for a contest.

To date there has not been one contest involving the speed camera in N.I. with or without a Solicitor.

This is an indication of how strong the evidence of the Speed Camera is viewed, or that no one has yet had a good enough case to contest it.

Can you beat the speed traps?

There are lots of detectors and diffusers on the market and they can cost anything from a few pounds to hundreds of pounds.

Most of them don't deliver the goods and some may be illegal.

Radar detectors

Now quite legal, the idea behind these detectors is simple. The device detects radar being used in the proximity and alerts the driver. The driver then ensures his speed is below the limit.

The problem is that the use of radar is not limited to the police.

Radar is now put to a multitude of commercial uses. The automatic opening doors at shops use radar. Traffic lights are increasingly using radar to monitor traffic rather than having to sink expensive pressure devices into the road only to have them dug up by the latest cable company.

The cool image of a desperado one step ahead of the law is dented somewhat after you have locked your brakes up for the third time outside yet another late-night convenience store.

Laser detectors

Now also legal, the laser detector seemed to be the logical step for electronics manufacturers after the radar detectors. Chasing the police's change of emphasis onto the Laser.

However, this did not make as much technological sense as it would first seem. Radar detectors relied on picking up excess microwaves coming down the road. Laser, however, uses a very narrow beam and the chances of picking up any excess is unlikely. Therefore, the laser detector probably will only sound when your speed is being checked and as the laser only takes a fraction of a second to obtain a reading it will be an expensive means of informing you that you have been caught!

Laser diffusers

Laser diffusers are at the expensive end of the market and as with any equipment of this type the manufacturers will not give you any guarantees. But more importantly than this, laser diffusers are on legally dicey ground.

The difference between diffusers and detectors is that the diffuser actually attempts to interfere with the police laser beam

– Bringing it into the realms of obstructing police in the execution of their duty. Heavy stuff for any motorist to consider getting involved in.

So as you are flying down the road with a dashboard more in common with the bridge of the Starship Enterprise than a Vauxhall Corsa and the inevitable happens – a police officer steps out to stop you, don't be expecting him or her to be overly impressed with your purchases.

Forget about that break you were hoping for!

INSURANCE

INSURANCE

You must inform your insurance company when you get penalty points.

If you fail to do so you may be committing a criminal offence.

Remember any large claim on your insurance is routinely investigated by one of the company's investigators. Should they find any discrepancies, they will refuse to pay any claim that you may make. They may cover a third party's claim.

Few people realise that insurance companies penalise drivers who are awarded points by increasing premiums from 4 points onwards as follows:

0 – 3 points   generally no increase in premium

4 – 6 points   10 – 15% increase in premium
                    some companies refuse cover

7 – 9 points   50 – 100% increase in premium
                    very few companies will offer cover

These figures relate to normal private vehicle insurance.

Occupational drivers (taxi drivers for instance) will find loading starting from the first points they get and increasing at a more severe rate than shown above.

MOBILE PHONES

MOBILE PHONES

Regulation 127 of the Highway Code states:

"Never use a hand-held mobile phone or microphone when driving."

Although the Highway Code is not law by itself, it is stated in law that any failure to observe a provision of the Code may constitute evidence of Careless or Dangerous Driving. It is not necessarily an offence but if caught by the police using your mobile phone whilst driving you could be facing the following charges:

• Careless Driving: 3-9 points at a Magistrates Court

• Dangerous Driving: mandatory 12 month disqualification at a Magistrates Court

If it is a minor infringement, however, police may issue a Non-Endorsable Ticket for not having proper control of your vehicle.

SPEED LIMITS

SPEED LIMITS

Everyone thinks they know the speed limits but you only have to scratch the surface to find that people know surprisingly little.

If your big plan is to say "But I didn't know officer". Forget it!

Take the time to think of the roads that you travel every day to work and check what the speed limits are on those roads. You might surprise yourself.

30 mph limit

In built-up or town areas the speed limit is 30mph. These areas are where the most penalty points are dished out.

Built-up area: "a good indicator is to look out for street lights".

• 30 mph zones do not normally have repeater signs

When you enter a new speed limit there are large speed limit signs."Repeater" signs are small speed limit signs placed along the road to act as a reminder.

• Most other speed limits have repeater signs every 100m

• If you don't see any presume it's a 30 mph speed limit.

MAX. PERMISSIBLE SPEED

CARS
CAR DERIVED VANS
(UP TO 2 TONNES)
MOTORCYCLES

SINGLE CARRIAGEWAY	60MPH
DUAL CARRIAGEWAY	70MPH
MOTORWAY	70MPH

ALL VEHICLES TOWING A
CARAVAN OR TRAILE

MAX. PERMISSIBLE SPEED	
SINGLE CARRIAGEWAY	50MPH
DUAL CARRIAGEWAY	60MPH
MOTORWAY	60MPH

BUSES AND COACHES

SINGLE CARRIAGEWAY	50MPH
DUAL CARRIAGEWAY	60MPH
MOTORWAY	70MPH

GOODS VEHICLES (not exceeding 7.5 tonnes max. laden weight)

SINGLE CARRIAGEWAY	50MPH
DUAL CARRIAGEWAY	60MPH
MOTORWAY	70MPH

GOODS VEHICLES (exceeding 7.5 tonnes max. laden weight)

SINGLE CARRIAGEWAY	40MPH
DUAL CARRIAGEWAY	50MPH
MOTORWAY	60MPH

ENDORSABLE
TICKET OFFENCES

ENDORSABLE TICKET OFFENCES

Speeding

• Know the speed limit for the road that you are on.

Sounds obvious, yet this is probably the most commonly used excuse by drivers caught speeding. When you pass a speed limit sign look at it!

• Look for the repeater signs approximately 100m apart. If there are no repeater signs you are probably in a 30 mph zone.

• When you approach a speed limit sign get down to that speed immediately

Especially a 30mph or a 40mph, these will have the most dangers and will have the highest degree of police enforcement. There is no "buffer zone" where you are allowed to continue to travel at a speed somewhere in between the two speed limits. Use your brakes. Don't coast.

Stopping on a motorway   3 Points

The most common way of getting yourself a ticket for this offence is thinking that you are being good and pulling onto the hard shoulder to take a call on your mobiles. However, the hard shoulder of a motorway is for emergencies only and that does not extend to

speaking to your loved ones or even getting that order you were after.

Breach of part-time bus lane M1 motorway   3 Points

This is the first such part-time bus lane on a Motorway in Europe. It's part of the Government's lead push to get drivers out of their cars and into public transport.

It has electric remotely operated signs informing the motorists and bus drivers when the bus way is in operation.

The bus way starts at the city-bound on-slip at Stockmans Lane and finishes at the Broadway Roundabout.

It is not only enforced by police patrols, it has, for the first time in N.I, static enforcement cameras.

Enforcement by this system will be operated in the same manner as the Speed Cameras. Offenders will receive a conditional offer in the post.

The normal operating hours are Mon–Fri 7.30–9.30AM but there are plans to extend these hours to include the evening peak hours.

Only buses designed to carry 28 seated passengers or more are permitted to use the bus way.

The bus way is also monitored by CCTV and should a vehicle break down it will still use the bus way and the bus way will then be suspended. The signs will then change reverting the bus way back to a hard shoulder.

Road markings: solid white lines 3 Points

When the solid white line is the line closest to you, it means you must not cross that line.

If the broken white line is the closest to you, you may cross the line; provided that you are able to complete your manoeuvre before it becomes solid on your side.

If they are both solid lines neither of you can cross.

There are exceptions to crossing the solid white line however:

• When you are turning right

• When you are passing a parked vehicle

• When overtaking a pedal cycle, horse or road maintenance vehicle if travelling at 10mph or less

Breach of red light 3 points

When the traffic light shows red you must stop behind the stop line (the solid white line).

If you are in a queue of traffic and have already crossed the stop line but have not cleared the junction when your traffic light turns to red, you are not in

breach of the light if you continue. However, it must be safe for you to drive on otherwise you might be committing another offence of Careless or Inconsiderate Driving (not an Endorsable Ticket but a court appearance, 3–9 points). Sometimes, it would be safer to stay stationary and allow traffic who have been given the green light to proceed. It's a judgement call.

Defective tyre   3 points

The legal minimum tread depth is at least 1.6mm throughout a continuous band comprising the central three quarters of the breadth of the tread and around the entire circumference of the tyre.

So, if you have a spot in the middle of the tyre that is below 1.6mm the tyre is defective.

This 1.6.mm minimum limit applies to

- cars

- minibuses with up to 8 seated passengers not including the driver

• motor vehicles and light trailers including caravans up to 3500kg gross vehicle weight.

A lot of motorists do not seem to realise that this law extends to trailers and caravans.

Checking the depth

There are some inexpensive gauges available to help you but the easiest method is using the "tyre wear indicators" which most makes of tyre now have. There are usually at least six small ribs across the bottom of the main tread grooves and when the tread surface becomes level with these ribs the tyre is at the legal limit and must be replaced.

The 1.6mm limit does not apply to motorcycles or large goods vehicles. They have a lower limit of 1mm. Offences can also relate to:

• Mixing: an incorrect mix of radial and cross-ply tyres

• Inflation: a tyre not inflated correctly for its purpose

• Cuts: certain long and deep cuts especially on the wall of the tyre making it prone to blow out

• Lumps, bulges or tears caused by separation or partial failure of the tyre structure.

Breach of signs

"Stop" — 3 Points

You must stop at the solid white line.

"No Entry" — 3 Points

Remember reversing into a "No Entry" is a breach of the sign, you may be facing in the right direction but it doesn't get you off!

'R' driver not displaying 'R' plates in prescribed manner — 2 points

This offence covers:

- Restricted Drivers not displaying their 'R' plates at all

- Restricted Drivers who decide that the 'R' plates lack credibility and cut down the white back-ground. The size of the 'R' plate, the 'R' and the white back ground are all stipulated in the legislation and any tampering with the size will leave you open to an Endorsable ticket.

Parking or stopping within the limits of a Pelican or Zebra Crossing — 3 points

Parking or stopping at these locations pose an obvious risk to pedestrians.

There is no exemption for vans or lorries delivering. We all know it can be very difficult for drivers of lorries and vans to deliver to shops in busy high streets, after all if they didn't deliver the goods we would not be able to buy them. Therefore, the police may permit parking on yellow lines and turn a blind eye to double parking but they usually draw the line at Pelican or Zebra Crossings.

A full list of endorsable ticket offences can be found in the Appendix.